Salute to the Potters

John Abberley

You don't often find pottery workers with a sense of self-importance. More likely, they'll say they've grown up with the job, or it runs in the family, or they can't do anything else. And the modesty is genuine. Yet the Staffordshire potters make products which have been admired and prized round the world for centuries.

No-one does it better and this needs to be said again and again when the industry is fighting for its life against foreign competition. The Potteries would be a strange place without the potbanks. Some, like Wedgwood and Spode, have been in business for well over 200 years. And for the most part, the workers have lived up to their reputation as the jolly potters. Women used to sing all day in the workshops. Perhaps this merriment and good humour had something to do with the kind of jobs they did.

A woman might have been a sponger, or a sticker-up, or even a stripper. There were other odd-sounding jobs like a jiggerer, a jolleyer, a ginnetter and, of course, a saggar-maker's bottom-knocker. That one famously beat the panel on the TV programme What's My Line? in the 1950s.

It's a dynastic kind of industry, with sons following fathers and daughters following mothers to the workbenches and the ovens. That goes for the bosses, too. Members of the same family ran companies from the beginning to the end. The relationships between bosses and workpeople created a family atmosphere all round. It wasn't unusual for someone to work at a potbank for 50 years. One old man at Tunstall was still at his bench on his 90th birthday. Even so, the pottery works of yesteryear was a grim place in some respects. Besides the smoking bottle ovens, workers used to be exposed to dangerous materials and ever-present dust. They died in thousands from dust disease or chest ailments under the general heading of "potter's rot". Countless inquests recorded death due to pneumoconiosis until factories were forced to comply with strict health regulations. Up to the 1950s, workers lived in houses cheek by jowl with the potbanks and children grew up in an atmosphere fouled by the blackest of smoke. No wonder the national image of Smoky Stoke lingered so long. It might not be dead even yet.

Yet local people like the artist Reginald Haggar and the photographer Ernest Warrillow found beauty and drama in the Potteries industrial scene and lovingly portrayed it for posterity. At the outset I suggested that pottery workers didn't regard themselves as important. That doesn't mean they had no pride in the job. Even when the conditions were terrible, they produced the finest

kind of ware. For the greater part of the 20th Century, North Staffordshire remained the world centre of the pottery trade, with a workforce of around 50,000 and up to 300 independent firms. But old traditions, like the old hand skills, came to an end.

After the disappearance of the bottle ovens and the smoke, the industry started to go downhill. Takeovers meant the end for many family firms and in two decades the workforce shrank to half its size. Employers used the new word "outsourcing" which signalled a switch to production overseas with cheaper labour. But although the pottery industry may be facing an uncertain future, we can celebrate the skill and dedication of the ordinary men and women who made the Potteries a household name across every continent. This book is a tribute to all of them.

The author gratefully acknowledges the assistance and photographs provided by the Potteries Museum, Ray Johnson, Roy Lewis and Jim Morgan.

The Way We Were
Salute to the Potters

Contents

Potters at Work

From potter's wheels to bottom-knockers, these pictures illustrate
the myriad work involved in pottery-making, particularly before
automation replaced traditional skills. It wasn't unusual for
generations of families to live out their working lives in the potbank
often under the same employer. Husbands and wives, fathers
and sons, mothers and daughters all helped to produce pottery
which ranked among the world's finest. Until the middle of the
20th century, the Potteries was still as grim as the place depicted
in Arnold Bennett's novels, but the working potters created beauty
amid the smoke and squalor.

A dipper at Shelley
Potteries, Fenton, with a
biscuitware plate after
dipping it in liquid glaze.
The plates on the board
are drying out

Pottery placers building towers of saggars inside an old bottle oven. These hollow
vessels, made of refractory material, protected ware from direct heat. A saggar was
often balanced on a man's head. The ladder was known to workers as the 'hoss'.

The job of making the ware may be finished, but it still requires the skill of the packer to send a consignment safely to its destination. This packer is carefully separating items of flatware before placing them in a bed of straw.

Children as young as 11 were still employed full-time in the pottery industry in the early 1900s. This group of workers in their early teens are seen 'carrying out', or taking products and materials from one department to another.

Old saggars were used to build a dividing wall at the back of two terraced houses in John Street, Longton, which was a notorious slum area in the early 1900s. Many houses like these were situated cheek by jowl with a pottery works.

A saggarmaker's bottom-knocker! It's the pottery job which famously beat the panel on the early television programme What's My Line. It was performed mostly by boys like these, pictured in the early 1900s. Two are holding the tools which knocked the bottom piece of the saggar firmly into place.

No saggars were required to protect the ware from heat in this enamel kiln, which was used for applying colour onto glaze. In the process of firing finely-decorated pieces, the temperature is much lower than that in a glost oven. The 1920s picture shows a kiln fireman at Enoch Wedgwood's works, Tunstall, placing ware on the shelves in small stands.

Before automatic processes took over from the paintbrush, freehand painting was a widespread skill among women pottery workers. This is a view of the painting shop at the old Wedgwood works in Etruria around 1930. Some decorating is still done in the traditional way on high-quality ware. The Sentinel buildings now stand on the site of the works.

One of Josiah Wedgwood's descendants, Hensleigh Wedgwood, seen at the wheel in a corner of the old Etruria factory where his illustrious ancestor once worked. Hemsley was one of two members of the family working there daily in 1930, when the company was preparing to celebrate the Wedgwood bicentenary.

Now you can see why they're called the jolly potters! Besides kicking out like chorus girls, these saggarmen were also demonstrating their traditonal art of balancing a saggar on the head. To make a flat surface, they made a ring of old stockings, known as a doughnut, and placed it beneath their hats.

Blunging — it's a good name for a basic job in the pottery industry which required workers to get their hands into a lot of wet and sticky clay. These men are seen operating a blunger, which mixed raw materials into the right consistency in preparation for making a clay body.

These Jasper plaques showing the Queen's head in white relief were commissioned to mark the 50th anniversary of the National Savings movement in 1966. Wedgwood ornamenter Fred Podmore is applying the Queen's portrait in clay onto the base of the plaque, taken from an original model by Arnold Machin.

How far automatic processes have revolutionised pottery making can be seen from this
picture of a cup sponging machine in operation at the Blyth factory of John Tams in Longton.
It was taken in 1974 when the firm was celebrating its centenary.

Girls and women carrying boards of pots on one shoulder used to be familiar sight in the potbank. These women at the old Wedgwood factory in Etruria were taking 'green' ware for inspection before its first firing.

A woman worker feeding cups into a direct screen printing machine at the Blyth factory of John Tams. With this and other machinery replacing the old hand skills, it explains why the term 'pottery operative' has come into general use.

The days of the saggar maker were coming to an end when Lewis Nixon posed for this picture at Acme Marls, Burslem, in 1968. Modern methods of firing meant the old-type saggar was no longer required. Mr Nixon did the job for nearly 50 years.

These women workers in the cup shop at Myott-Meakin, Cobridge, were all smiles when the factory reopened in September 1980 only three months after a closedown. The firm was bought from its previous owners by a consortium of businessmen, saving 170 jobs.

Writers might have been less than complimentary about the Potteries landscape, but even J B Priestley had kind things to say about the pretty pottery girls. They could certainly have applied to this trio at the John Tams factory, Longton, who were celebrating the firm's success in winning the Queen's Award for export achievement in 1987.

When it comes to throwing a pot, the basics haven't changed very much since Josiah Wedgwood practised the art at Etruria from 1769. This picture of a thrower's hands carefully shaping a vase was taken nearly two centuries later.

Steady does it! A placer passing a saggar to a colleague inside an already well-filled oven. A good sense of balance and a head for heights were both essential qualities to do the job. The picture was taken in 1930.

This aircraft was brought into service when a London restaurant sent an SOS for coffee cups and saucers to be delivered for a banquet. The call was made one afternoon in 1953 to the Longton firm of Collingwood China, one of 10 firms sharing a plane based at the old Meir Airport. The large consignment of ware reached the London restaurant 90 minutes after the take-off from Meir.

One of the scores of marlholes which once pitted the Potteries landscape. This one, pictured by the pioneer photographer W J B Blake, was close to the centre of Longton. The railway track was used to haul raw clay to the surface.

Wicker baskets were used for packing china for most of the 20th century until they were replaced by modern containers. In this 1914 picture the ware is being placed in crates packed with straw. Both packing and crate making were skilled jobs.

The Longton company of Hewitt and Leadbetter made ceramic dolls' heads from 1914 at the Willow Pottery. They sold well on the toy market. The women on this old postcard were applying colours to the tiny faces.

Bottle Ovens & Factories

When outsiders talk about the Staffordshire Potteries, many still think of a skyline crowded with bottle ovens and chimneys. In truth, that smoky national image disappeared as long ago as the 1960s after new firing processes had made the old ovens redundant. Nowadays there are only 40-odd of them left to remind the present generation of how it was in their grandparents' day when smoke poured from 2,000 bottle ovens.

A view of the ovens at the Falcon Works in Sturgess Street, Stoke, taken during the 1976 survey. They were formerly part of the Goss Works, a noted name in the pottery industry in the early part of the 20th century.

One of a series of postcards which helped to create the national image of the Potteries as 'Smoky Stoke'. This one from around 1910 shows a view across Longton and is ironically captioned "Fresh air for the Potteries".

An aerial view of the large Simpson's Works, located next door to the Roman Catholic Church in Waterloo Road, Cobridge. The picture, taken in the 1930s, shows the company's variety of bottle ovens. Simpson's are still in business today.

Dolby's Mill, standing beside the Trent and Mersey Canal at Stoke, was a familiar sight to thousands of passing motorists on the A500. The works, which was engaged in calcining flint, ceased production around 1966.

It could almost be Venice, but rather less romantically, this classic frontage was part of the Royal Doulton sanitaryware works off Whieldon Road, Stoke. Situated close to the old Stoke City football ground, the factory was formerly owned by Winkle and Wood and known as the Colonial Pottery.

The entrance to the 18th-century Bell Pottery is near the centre of this picture, taken at the top of Broad Street, Hanley. In 1940 the old works was still making pottery, but by 1950 it was unused and the first stage of the Potteries Museum was built on the site. All the business premises facing the street were demolished.

A working boat on the Caldon Canal pictured alongside J and G Meakin's Eastwood Pottery, Hanley, with a classic set of bottle ovens as the background. The company, formed by two brothers in the 19th century, was taken over by Johnson Brothers and later became part of the Wedgwood group.

The Old Foley Pottery in King Street, Fenton, was built in 1790 by Josiah Spode for his son Samuel. It passed through the hands of several owners and James Kent Ltd took over around 1900. The works has continued to produce pottery up to the end of the 20th century.

The famous pottery name of Coalport China originated in Shropshire in 1750, but the firm was transferred to Shelton in 1926 when it was taken over by Cauldon Potteries. This Coalport factory in King Street, Fenton, photographed in 1973, has been replaced by modern premises as part of the Wedgwood group, which acquired Coalport in 1967.

These huge 19th-century bottle ovens at the Ridgway Pottery, Shelton, were claimed to be the largest in the area. During the Second World War they were used as air raid shelters. They were demolished in the 1960s.

Ashworth's chimney dominated this view over the rooftops from a window of the Potteries Museum in 1961. The Hanley earthenware factory of Geo L Ashworth dated back to 1815 and the firm's roots went back to the 18th century. The chimney and buildings were demolished a few years after the picture was taken. Just visible is the top of the Mitchell Memorial Theatre with its porthole windows.

This wall mural in a Hanley shop became widely known as the front cover of Fred Leigh's best-selling book, Sentinel Street. It represents a scene from 1900 in Century Street (formerly Brook Street), Hanley, and incorporates the factories of Newhall Pottery, Peel Pottery and Clarence Street Pottery.

This part of the famous Minton Works at London Road, Stoke, was in a delapidated state when photographed in 1965 shortly before demolition. The bottle ovens had previous been hidden from view by tall buildings fronting the roadway.

The renowned Moorcroft Pottery at Cobridge, seen in 1936 when the firm still had its full complement of slim bottle ovens. Now only one remains as part of the Moorcroft showroom.

Postcard view of canalside potbanks at Middleport before the First World War. This section of the Trent and Mersey Canal was a 'port' for Burslem firms. On the right are piles of materials landed by canal boats and where the canal bends are the premises of the Mersey Weaver Company, general carriers.

Swans give a touch of romance to this canalside scene at Meakin's wharf off Lichfield Street, Hanley, in 1965. The bottle ovens were known to workers and locals as the Seven Sisters, although not all of them can seen on the picture.

The delapidated and empty Greengates Pottery of William Adams at Tunstall, one of the industry's great names. The firm's 18th-century founder was a strong competitor with Josiah Wedgwood by 1790, producing fine jasper ware at the Greengates Works. Later, Adams ware was also made at the Greenfield factory until this production was transferred to the enlarged older works in 1956. Latterly, this became part of the Wedgwood group before the works was closed and demolished.

An angler fishing in the canal at Barlaston, not by the light of the moon but in the bright reflections from the Wedgwood factory, silhouetted against the autumn sky. Wedgwood moved to Barlaston from the old Etruria works in 1940. The picture was taken in 1970.

An early Victorian print showing Enoch Wood's Fountain Place Works in Burslem. The factory, with its mixture of architectural styles, dated back to 1789. The large building on the right has survived to the present day.

A shrub growing out of the side of a long-disused bottle oven in Sutherland Road, Longton, in 1967. By that time the firing of pottery kilns with coal was forbidden by pollution laws. A total of 44 ovens were saved from demolition, but this wasn't one of them.

The middle one of these three pottery ovens at Acme Marls, Burslem, had the distinction of being the last commercially-fired bottle oven of all. This happened in October 1977 with a ceremony which saw a flame lit from the oven taken by horse-drawn coach to ignite a tunnel kiln at the new Acme Marls works at Tunstall.

A wintry scene outside the Myott-Meakin factory in Crane Street, Cobridge, fitted the mood of the workers in June 1980. The American-owned earthenware firm had just announced hundreds of redundancies due to Far East competition.

Before it was taken over for pottery manufacture, the part of this building nearest the camera was Burslem Workhouse. Situated in Wedgwood Place in the town centre, it was occupied for many years by the firm of Alcock, Lindley and Bloore. The factory was demolished in 1956.

On the evidence of this scene, there was still a strong pottery presence in Tunstall in the 1950s. In the foreground was a group of bottle ovens at Dudson's factory, with a further dozen on the far left belonging to the firms of W H Grindley and Williamsons. The tinpot-lid roof of the Sacred Heart Roman Catholic Church stands out in the right background

In 1976 three types of bottle oven were still standing together at the Campbell Tile Company in London Road, Stoke. They were (left to right) calcining, circular and double square. Sixty ovens were surveyed by the North Staffs Junior Chamber of Commerce to make a permanent record for the Gladstone Pottery Museum.

A close-up view of the Falcon Pottery ovens in 1989, showing the extent of decay and dereliction. At that time they were part of the Portmeirion Works and facing demolition.

Even in the 1930s, some pottery workers still lived in small and insanitary houses under the shadow of the factories and bottle ovens. This typical scene, long vanished, was in St Martin's Lane, Longton. One visiting writer described it as "Victorian industrialism in its dirtiest and most cynical aspect".

Pottery workers at a Tunstall factory waiting at the works entrance for the arrival of King George V and Queen Mary on their first visit to the area in 1913. It was the custom of the day to erect a decorated arch and banner for special occasions. The royal couple's two-day tour covered the Potteries, Newcastle and Leek. They stayed with the Marquis of Crewe at Crewe Hall.

Classic picture of narrowboat passing the bottle ovens of J and G Meakin alongside the Caldon Canal in Hanley. It was taken around 1930 and the man on the towpath has been identified as Ernie Gorton, who worked for the Anderton Canal Carrying Company. As captain of an Anderton boat, he was known as a knobstick. He was starting on the long journey to Runcorn with a cargo of pottery for export. Going in the opposite direction, the boats carried clay, flint and stones to factories.

The end was near for the Edensor Works of Elektra Porcelain when these bottle ovens — claimed to be largest in Longton — were photographed in 1973. The company, founded in 1924, produced earthenware entitled Zanobia, Vulcan and Cellulose. Royal Doulton took over shortly before the firm closed in 1971.

A ceremonial last firing of a bottle oven, organised by the Gladstone Pottery Museum, took place at the Hudson and Middleton Works, Longton, in 1978. The man in charge was veteran pottery manufacturer Alfred Clough, seen here relaxing beside one of the mouths. A range of commemorative ware was fired.

Twyfords sanitaryware is known in bathrooms all round
the world and this is where it was made from the 1950s.
The modern factory at Cliffe Vale was built only a short
distance from the original Twyford works, now converted
into flats. The company opened another new factory at
Alsager. The company was later taken over by Caradon.
The firm's founder, Thomas Twyford, was chairman of
directors at the Sentinel for many years when the newspaper
was independently owned.

Smoke billowing out across the nearby Shelton Cemetery from one of a large group of bottle ovens at Twyford's sanitaryware works, Cliffe Vale. Ernest Warrillow's 1951 picture was used as the backdrop to the opening title of the long-running Clayhanger series on ATV.

It seems inconceivable that the huge Dimmocks pottery works once dominated the area now called Hanley's Cultural Quarter. It was bounded by Stafford Street, Piccadilly, Cheapside and Albion Square. The tall chimney was demolished in 1905 in front of a large crowd.

An potworks of the late 17th century, part of a farmstead, as illustrated by Dr Robert Plot in his book The Natural History of Staffordshire. The man on the right is mixing slip.

Josiah Wedgwood's original 18th-century works on the banks of the Trent and Mersey Canal at Etruria. The picture, taken around 1900, shows the factory on the same level as the canal before it subsided by at least 10 feet.
The Round House on the left is the only preserved fragment of the old works, which was demolished in the 1960s.

Royal Visits, Pottery Queens and Celebrations

Up to the Second World War, royal visitors were rarely seen in the potbanks, although during the 1920s the Wedgwood works at Etruria welcomed two princes in the space of six weeks. However, in post-war decades royals came on a regular basis, particularly Princess Margaret during her 30 years' association with Keele University. Queen Elizabeth and Prince Philip have been among the pottery workers on several occasions, creating an atmosphere of delightful informality, as did Prince Charles on his visits.

In this chapter there are pictures of the old-style 'Pottery Queens' chosen from the many pretty girls at the workbenches. The first queen was crowned in 1934 and the event continued until well into the 1960s. Harking back to 1930, I have included pictures of the week-long Wedgwood bicentenary celebrations, probably the biggest event ever staged by a single company in North Staffordshire.

In a demonstration to prove the strength of bone china, a three and a half ton lorry stands a few inches above the ground supported by four Wedgwood teacups. In the driving seat is Sir John Wedgwood, deputy chairman of the company. Tower Bridge makes an impressive background for this 1958 picture.

Queen Mary watching a pottery worker during her visit to Wedgwood's factory at Etruria in July 1939. After her tour of the factory the Queen Mother visited the site of the new Wedgwood works and garden village being built at Barlaston.

Queen Mary meeting a guest during her tour of the Wedgwood works in 1939. She was presented with items of Jasper ware by Josiah Wedgwood, a descendant of the founder, as a memento of the visit.

With the cheers of the 1000-strong workforce in her ears, Queen Mary got into the royal Daimler at the end of her visit to the Wedgwood works at Etruria. She carried the walking-stick which she used on her tour of the factory.

A portrait plate dominates this group of four items produced by Royal Doulton to commemorate the 90th birthday of the Queen Mother. On the left is a hand-made figure and on the right are a Royal Crown Derby loving cup and a crystal goblet.

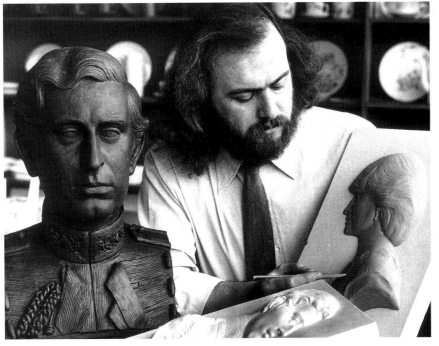

After the engagement of Prince Charles and Lady Diana Spencer was announced in 1981, Wedgwood chief modeller Mike Dillon worked overtime to produce plaque moulds of the royal couple. Cameos of the moulds were reproduced on a selection of Jasper ware. On the table beside Mike is a black basalt bust of Princes Charles which was modelled by David McFall.

Paragon, another Longton china firm, made a traditional loving cup to celebrate the 25th anniversary Queen's coronation. The lion handles were finished in gold and other decorations included a rose, thistle, shamrock and daffodil.

What was the big joke? The camera caught a light-hearted moment during a visit by Prince Charles to the Coloroll factory at Meir. The Prince was clearly tickled by something said during his conversation with gilder Glenda Bennett.

Prince Charles looked impresssed by Coloroll's gift of a large loving cup to commemorate his visit to the Meir factory.

Everything was laid out for dinner when the Duke of Edinburgh toured the Spode Copeland stand at the Brussels trade fair in 1958. With managing director Spencer Copeland looking on, the Duke smiled his approval.

In the aftermath of the death of King George VI in 1952, the Queen Mother and Princess Margaret were regularly seen together at public engagements. Here they were visiting the Wedgwood stand at the 1953 British Industrial Fair at Olympia. They were inspecting the Golden Persephone dinner set, which was chosen for the coronation banquet that year. Chatting with the royal couple was Felton Wreford, Wedgwood's London manager.

Princess Margaret welcomed to the Hanley group of Johnson Brothers in 1966 by the chairman of the company, Sir Ernest Johnson.

It was a moment to treasure for three 'Doulton Dollies' when they met the Queen Mother at the International Spring Fair in Birmingham. The girls on the stand were (left to right) Leslie Young, Janet Hanley and Debra Birtles.

A board of half-finished cups caught Princess Margaret's eye during her visit to Johnson Brothers. She took one off carefully for examination, watched by general manager John Cope and joint managing director Basil Johnson.

A smiling Queen Mother was pleased with the range of tableware on show on the Royal Doulton stand at the National Exhibition Centre in Birmingham. Pictured with her were managing director Richard Bailey and George Bott, chief executive of the firm's domestic ware sales division.

A line of pottery ladies in smart overalls waved Union Jacks to greet the Queen on her arrival at the former Mason's Ironstone China in Hanley in 1973. During her tour the Queen was accompanied by the firm's chairman, J S Goddard.

A handshake from the Duke of Gloucester for fettler Lily Povey during the Duke's tour of the new Longton works, which was built on the site in Sutherland Road of the former Barker Brothers factory.

There was a royal opening for the John Tams group's Sutherland factory at Longton by the Duke of Gloucester. He is seen (on left) inside the new works with group chairman, Gerald Tams, great-grandson of the firm's founder, and Mrs Tams, a fellow director.

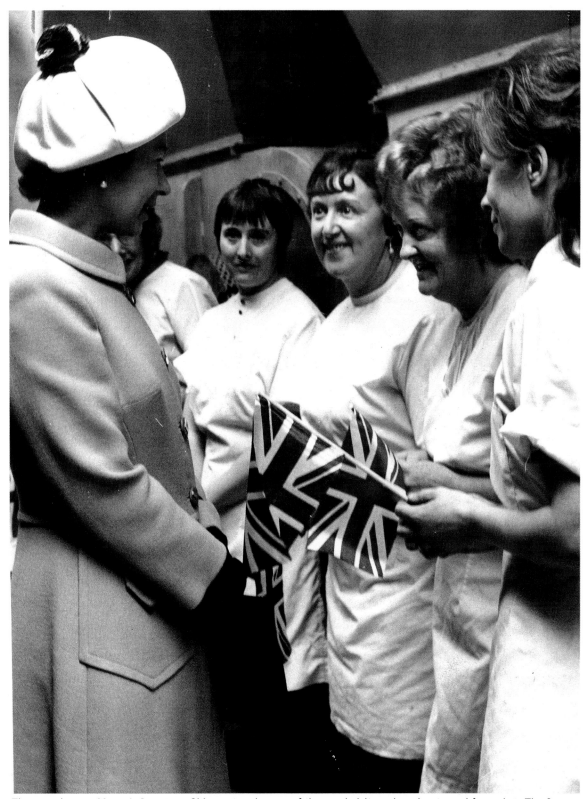

These workers at Mason's Ironstone China got a close-up of the royal visitor when she stopped for a chat. The Queen, accompanied by the Duke of Edinburgh, stayed at the old Hanley factory for 45 minutes.

It was the darkest time of the Second World War when King George VI and Queen Elizabeth paid a brief visit to the Potteries in February 1941 as part of a nationwide tour to boost morale. The royal couple called at the Spode Copeland works in Stoke where they were greeted by an enthusiastic crowd in the courtyard.

The Duke of Edinburgh in an earnest exchange with a group of male employees at Mason's Ironstone China. The factory, which became part of the Wedgwood group, has since been demolished.

Long-serving Spode employees pictured in close encounters with the royal visitors, who were accompanied during their tour by the company chairman, Ronald Copeland, seen on the extreme right.

Rene Shipley faces the cameras with her retinue before being crowned the 1937 Pottery Queen in Hanley Park. She began as a paintress at the Spode Copeland works in Stoke and later transferred to the wages department. She was given a brooch, made by Pidducks the jewellers, bearing the arms of Stoke-on-Trent.

A salute from King George VI to cheering workers at the conclusion of the royal visit to Spode Copeland in February 1941. The King and Queen also visited Shelton Steelworks.

In the space of six weeks in 1924, two future kings toured the Wedgwood works at Etruria. The Duke of Windsor (later King Edward VIII) was followed by the Duke of York (later King George VI), who was pictured examining a tea service.

Clarice Cliff's workers called themselves the Bizarre girls after the designer's patterns.
This picture shows them in comic costumes when they took part in a carnival in 1931.

Dressed in morning coat and tails, Shepard Johnson interested the Queen in a particular piece of Johnson Brothers earthenware in the showroom. A fellow director, Basil Johnson, is in the background.

Staffordshire girls are fair, runs an old rhyme, and that has certainly been true of many working in the pottery industry. A beauty contest to find the first Pottery Queen was held in 1934 when Annie Sheppard was crowned in Hanley Park. Annie, employed at George Jones's Crescent Pottery in Stoke, was chosen from hundreds of entrants.

Finalists in the first Pottery Queen contest pictured after the judging at Trentham Gardens in 1934. The winner, Annie Sheppard, is seated centre. The event attracted a crowd of several thousand people.

Honorary degress conferred by Princess Margaret at Keele University in 1983 included one for Richard Bailey, Royal Doulton Tableware's chief executive. He was awarded the degree of Master of the University.

Becky Calder in her finery after being crowned the 1938 Pottery Queen. One of three sisters from Etruria, Becky worked at Weatherby's Pottery in Hanley. She later ran a florist's shop at Kidsgrove.

BECKY CALDER
POTTERY QUEEN, 1938-39

The bicentenary of Josiah Wedgwood's birth in 1930 was celebrated with a week-long pageant centred on Hanley Park. In this picture characters in pageant costumes mingle with the huge crowd outside Hanley town hall before moving off in procession.

A tableau called The Dancing Hours performed by children at the Wedgwood bicentenary pageant in 1930.

A festival of queens at Hanley Park which preceded the Pottery Queen crowning ceremony in the early 1950s. It's thought that the annual competition continued until 1964 when Edna Newnes was chosen as the last queen.

Roman soldiers marching in a procession heading for
Hanley Park during the Wedgwood bicentenary pageant.

George Bernard Shaw was
a surprise visitor to the
Wedgwood bicentenary
pageant in 1930. The
renowned writer is seen
here standing beside Lady
Joseph, wife of the North
Staffordshire industrialist
Sir Francis Joseph. She
was the pageant queen.

Celebrations in the lithographing shop at the Wharf Pottery of Wood and Sons, Burslem, to mark the coronation of King George VI in 1937. Mrs Jean Keeling recalls that she often visited her mother in the workshop. Factory regulations, she says, were more relaxed then than they are today.

King George V acknowledges the cheering workers as he and Queen Mary cross the yard at the Spode Works of W T Copeland and Sons, Stoke, in 1913. Walking beside the Queen is the young Ronald Copeland, grandson of the firm's founder.

Pottery Designs and Artists

From Susie Cooper to Roy Midwinter, pottery designers in Staffordshire have given a lead to the rest of the world. Josiah Wedgwood did the same with his Portland Vase, though he produced only a small number in the first edition of 1789. In this chapter you'll find some of the finest and most distinctive pottery designs of the 20th century and, as a form of light relief, examples of ware made specially for children. This section also highlights another kind of contribution to the pottery industry – by landscape artists who have put past industrial scenes on canvas for posterity. The paintings include works by Reginald Haggar, the acknowledged master of the genre, and several other local artists. As you might expect, the bottle ovens loom large among the pictures.

This fine 19th-century piece of ornamental earthenware depicts bull-baiting, which was a popular sport less than two centuries ago. It was made at Obadiah Sherratt's factory in Burslem around 1830 and painted in enamel colours.

It might only have been a humble chamber pot to slide under the bed, but decorating it was still a work of art to this paintress. She is seen at the Bradwell Works of Arthur Wood and Son in 1971. Americans are known to purchase a chamber pot to distribute crisps at parties.

Not a foreign-made pot in sight! Woolworths were obviously happy to encourage their customers to buy British when this consignment of Staffordshire pottery went on display. This was in the days before decimalisation when you could buy a 12-piece decorated bone china teaset for 27 shillings (£1.35).

A handy reminder of the reigns and dates of all the kings and queens of England was provided by Longton china manufacturers Aynsley in 1978. The ornamental mugs and trays were made to commemorate the 25th anniversary of the coronation of Queen Elizabeth II.

Reverse view of Josiah Wedgwood's Portland Vase. The original vase, excavated from a grave near Rome in the 17th century, was smashed to pieces in 1845. However, it was restored with the help of Wedgwood's copy, which was used as the model.

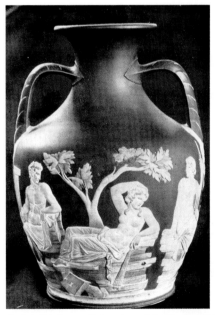

Josiah Wedgwood's version of the Portland Vase with figures in bas-relief, one of the finest examples of the potter's art to be found anywhere in the world. Wedgwood made it at Etruria in 1789 after borrowing the original vase in ornamental glass from the Duke of Portland. The first edition was limited to about two dozen copies.

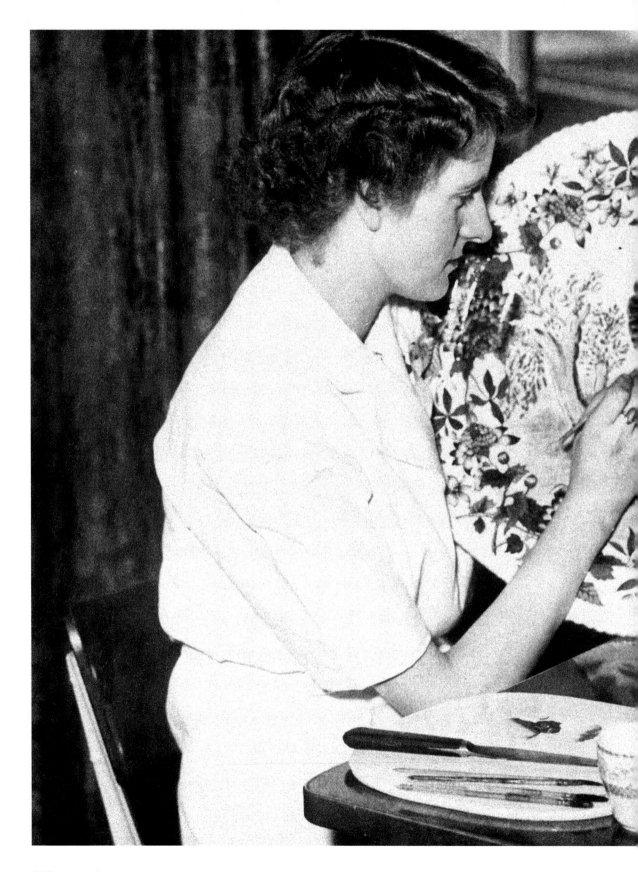

Much of the finest Spode Copeland ware has always been aimed at the American market. At a London exhibition in 1953, 19-year-old paintress Beryl Sidlet was pictured working on a turkey dish for the United States Thanksgiving.

Susie Cooper with an array of her patterns in 1982 when she was still working as a freelance designer with Wedgwood, based at the Tunstall works of William Adams. In 1979 she was awarded the OBE and in 1987 was awarded an honorary doctorate by the Royal College of Art. Miss Cooper (in private life Mrs Cecil Barker) died in 1995, aged 93.

In the 1950s Roy Midwinter took the pottery industry by storm with bright and bold designs which made his Burslem firm the most innovative pottery manufacturer in Staffordshire. He was helped by a team of designers comprising the Marquis of Queensberry, Terence Conran, the architect Sir Hugh Casson and the conservationist Peter Scott. Roy is pictured with designs which included a piece of oven-to-tableware designed by Conran and a plaque designed by Casson.

Distinguished artist Reginald Haggar captures part of the scene at the old Wedgwood works at Etruria in 1965 before the site was cleared. Mr Haggar was art director at Mintons before being appointed master-in-charge at Burslem School of Art. He was a world authority on ceramics.

A view of the Wedgwood factory at Etruria a hundred years ago, as depicted by Anthony Forster, a popular artist who has established a reputation for his old-time North Staffordshire scenes.

Wellknown Reginald Haggar
painting of Dolby's Mill in
the centre of Stoke.
The Potteries Museum has a
large collection of Haggar
paintings.

Reginald Haggar at the easel with one of his many watercolours depicting bottle ovens.
After the artist's death in 1988, the Potteries Museum launched an annual Reginald
Haggar lecture.

Pottery paintings by Reginald Haggar went on show at Stafford art gallery in 1971. Here the artist is caught in contemplative mood beside one of his pictures.

Smoking bottle ovens reflected in the waters of the Trent and Mersey Canal at Etruria. This is one of scores of paintings of the Potteries industrial scene of yesteryear by Alf Wakefield, a self-taught artist who was formerly a foreman electrician at Shelton Steelworks.

A builder's yard at Longton hard by a potbank which artist Alf Wakefield thinks may have been part of the Gladstone China Works. In the background is the tower of St James's Church.

Famous 18th-century painting by George Stubbs of Josiah Wedgwood with his wife Sarah and their family in the grounds of Etruria Hall.

Retired Sentinel artist Maurice Hancock demonstrated his penchant for fine detail with this view of a corner of the old Wedgwood Works at Etruria in the early 1900s. This is what Josiah Wedgwood called the 'useful' works, as opposed to their ornamental section. The bottle ovens were built in 1769 at the same time as the factory, making them nearly 200 years old when they were demolished in the 1960s.

Maurice Hancock's faithful reproduction, virtually brick by brick, of the long-demolished Parks Works, which stood next door to the Gladstone Pottery Museum at Longton. The ovens on the right with funnel chimneys were frit kilns, where raw materials like hard flint were prepared. The factory dated back to 1832.

Sir George Wade, chairman and father-figure of the Wade group at Burslem, at work with his paintbrushes at his home, Brand Hall, Norton in Hales, near Market Drayton. In his retirement he devoted a lot of time to his interest in art.

EILEEN SOPER
Childrens' China
by PARAGON

Firms large and small have been involved in making pottery for children and famous designers like Clarice Cliff and Susie Cooper expressed their talent in nurseryware, as did book illustrators like Beatrix Potter and Mabel Lucie Attwell. Paragon China, of Longton, placed this advertisement for nursery ware by the artist Eileen Soper in the Pottery Gazette in 1936.

Ding Dong Bell, a children's nursery rhyme mug produced by Arthur Wood and Sons, Burslem, in the 1940s.

Early-to-bed plate from a children's teaset designed by E Radford and made by J H Cope and Co, Wellington China, Longton, in the 1930s.

Tableware set for a feast! Part of the banqueting service made by Spode Copeland in the early 19th century for Sir John Lubbock. Its hundreds of pieces represented an entire library of botanical patterns. In 1965 it was sold at Sotheby's for £4,500.

A study in concentration as designer Eve Midwinter puts the final touches to a coffee pot with a pattern called Denim. It was part of an oven-to-tableware set in Midwinter's Stoneware collection, designed by Robin Welch and Roy Midwinter. The picture was taken in 1979 when Midwinter was part of the Wedgwood group.

Terence Conran, later the founder of Habitat, designed a plate with a medley of vegetables while working for Roy Midwinter at Burslem in the 1950s.

Showrooms across the Potteries displayed ornamental tableware commemorating the coronation of King George VI in 1937. This particularly fine selection included pieces showing the King and Queen and the two princesses.

Millions of commemorative mugs were produced by the pottery industry to mark the coronation of King George VI in 1937. These women workers were sorting through a batch of ware which was mostly distributed to schoolchildren.

This 'television set' is a late example of Clarice Cliff's flair for original shapes and designs. The earthenware lap plate and cup by A J Wilkinson was from the late 1950s.

A set of baby's plates by Shelley's China, of Fenton, commemorating (left to right) the coronations of George VI in 1937, George V in 1911, and the uncrowned Edward VIII in 1937.

Enoch Wedgwood and Co, of Tunstall, produced this arresting pattern in kitchenware in 1957.

Another Potteries artist dedicated to bottle ovens was Harry Smith, whose subject in this work was the derelict Old Blue Bell Works in 1979. Harry, who taught art at Thistley Hough School, Penkhull, ran the Pentagon Gallery in Hanley for some years. He worked mainly in acrylics.

Do these pieces look like vases or paper handkerchiefs? They were produced by Arthur Wood and Son, Burslem, in the late 1950s.

Pottery Personalities

There was never any shortage of individual characters in an industry which thrived on the 'family feeling' in the potbank. One was undoubtedly Leslie Sillitoe, who rose from humble beginnings as a mouldmaker to become leader of the Ceramic and Allied Trades Union. Another was Sir George Wade, who remained as chairman of the Wade Group at Burslem until he was 79. In this chapter they are joined by a selection of other prominent people who left their mark on the pottery industry, including the famous designers Clarice Cliff, Susie Cooper and Charlotte Rhead. And who was the 13-year-old girl potter known as the Potteries Prodigy? Find her and all the rest in the following pages.

The little chap depicted on the statuette was Tommy Greenleaves, who worked as a carter for J and G Meakin, Hanley, for 50 years. This character, who has became part of the folklore of the industry, slept above the horses in the works stables. He always wore a grey jacket fastened with one button. Pictured in 1982 holding the figure of Tommy was company chairman Derek Jones. A number of the statuettes were made in the 1920s.

A black basalt plaque of Five Towns novelist Arnold Bennett was modelled by Wedgwood chief designer Eric Owen, pictured with the plaque in 1960. It was placed in Burslem as a public memorial to the author.

As part of the Wedgwood bicentenary celebrations in 1959, the company staged an exhibition at Selfridge's Store in London. Deputy chairman Sir John Wedgwood was flanked by L B Harris, Selfridge's deputy manager, and Arthur Bryan, then the firm's London representative. Displaying her work was ornamenter Mrs M Roberts.

Harold Holdway, art director at Spode Copeland, showing off his designs marking Britain's entry into the European Common Market in 1972. On the plaque countries in the EEC were shaded in a dark colour.

One of the success stories of the pottery industry in post-war years has been the rise of Portmeirion Potteries. The firm was founded in 1960 by Sir Clough Williams-Ellis in the former Kirkham works at Stoke. It has been developed by his daughter, Susan Williams-Ellis, pictured with a soup tureen she designed and modelled herself. In the background is Portmeirion holiday village in North Wales, which her father also created. Susan studied art under the sculptor Henry Moore.

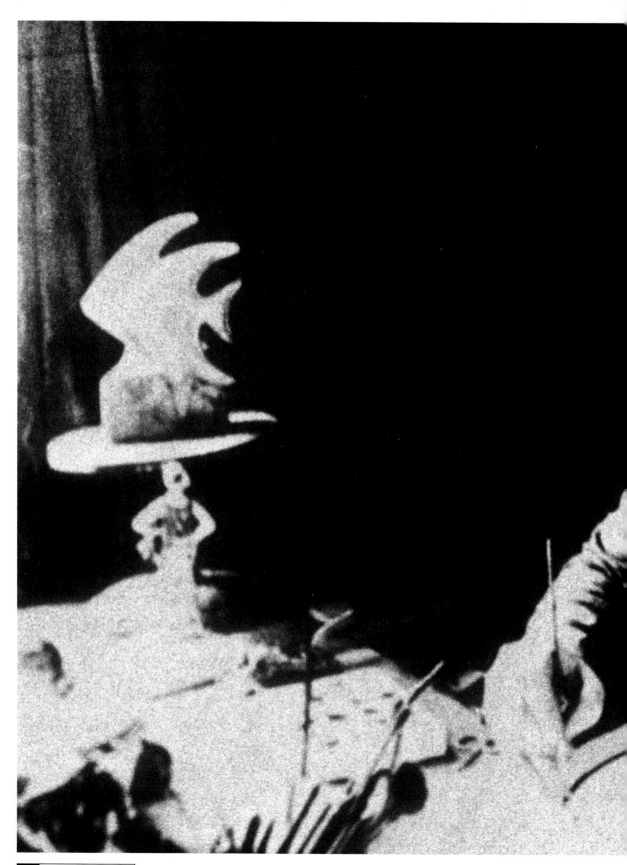

Clarice Cliff, one of the biggest names in pottery design in the 20th century, pictured in her studio at the Newport Pottery, Middleport, in the 1930s. She rose to fame with her Bizarre range of brightly-decorated and outlandishly-shaped ware. Today, her pieces which sold for sixpence or a shilling are worth four-figure sums.

With Clarice Cliff and Susie Cooper, Charlotte Rhead was the third member of a celebrated triumvirate of women pottery designers. The three appeared together on a televison documentary called The Pottery Ladies in 1985. Charlotte's speciality was tube-lining, an operation similar to icing a cake. Among others, she worked for Wood and Sons at Burslem, Burgess and Leigh at Middleport and A G Richardson's Gordon Pottery at Tunstall.

Roy Midwinter and his wife Eve looking at a collection of stoneware which the Burslem firm of Midwinter and Sons exhibited in London in 1979. The company had been formed in 1910, but by 1979 it was a member of the Wedgwood group. In the 1950s Roy Midwinter employed people on design work who later became famous, including Terence Conran. His wife Eve was also a leading pottery designer. Later, the couple were divorced.

The career of Sir Arthur Bryan with Josiah Wedgwood and Sons is a classic story of local boy makes good. A native of Penkhull, he left Longton High School at 16 and took his first job as a wartime bank worker at Trentham. After joining Wedgwood in 1947 he held various management posts both at home and overseas before becoming managing director. He was the company's first chief executive outside the Wedgwood family. Appointed chairman of the much-expanded group in 1968, Sir Arthur was president of Waterford Wedgwood on his retirement in 1988.

The boss was in the workplace when Richard Bailey was pictured at Royal Doulton's Nile Street Works at Burslem in 1982. At that time he was chief executive of Royal Doulton Tableware, having joined his uncle Cuthbert Bailey at Doultons in 1950. Later, as technical director, he led the team which won the Queen's Award for the development of English translucent china. He became chairman in 1980 and retired seven years later.

It was inevitable that Colonel Sir George Wade should be called the grand old man of the pottery industry. He didn't retire as chairman of the Wade group at Burslem until he was 79 and then pursued many other interests right up to his death at 94. A man with a caring interest in others, particularly his employees, Sir George also had a reputation as a humorous after-dinner speaker. He won the MC and bar for gallantry in the First World War.

As one of Stoke-on-Trent's surprisingly few lord mayors from the pottery industry, Les Sillitoe was immortalised in clay in 1982 by sculptor Colin Melbourne. Busts from the head were made in bronze and ceramics and put on display at Stoke town hall and in a London exhibition.

Wedgwood paid a tribute in gold to Sam Jerrett when he retired as director of the British Ceramic Manufacturers' Federation in 1984. Wedgwood chairman Sir Arthur Bryan presented him with a gold-inscribed commemorative mug. Also in this picture are (left to right) Christopher Johnson, deputy chairman Peter Williams, Fred de Costobadie, James Moffat and Robert Johnson.

Leslie Sillitoe rose from humble beginnings as a mouldmaker to become leader of the Ceramic and Allied Trades Union at a time when it had 40,000 members. As a union negotiator, he earned the title of peacemaker. He also served as Lord Mayor of Stoke-on-Trent and was awarded the OBE for his public work. A wartime soldier, he was founder chairman of the city branch of the Normandy Veterans' Association.

Prime Minister Edward Heath admiring a statuette of the first Josiah Wedgwood in 1971. He was calling at the Wedgwood stand at a London exhibition of new designs. The figure was a miniature replica of the 19th-century statue of Josiah Wedgwood which stands outside Stoke Station. It made in a limited edition of 2,000 copies.

Potting was very much a family business for Sir Ernest Johnson, who joined his father in the firm of Johnson Brothers in 1899 and subsequently introduced his own sons into the company. He was still joint managing director when he was over 80. During his time Johnsons was the largest earthenware manufacturer in the world. Apart from his prominence in industry, Sir Ernest played cricket for Staffordshire and was president of Stoke City FC. He died in 1962.

In 1987 there was a further honour for retired Royal Doulton chief Richard Bailey when he was made a freeman of the city of Stoke-on-Trent. He received the framed award from Lord Mayor Gordon Tuck. Also in the picture are council leader Ron Southern and chief executive Stewart Titchener.

Ronald Copeland, former head of Spode Copeland, wearing his other hat as a scout commissioner. He lived at Kibblestone Hall, near Stone, and in 1927 allowed scouts to use his land for camping. This eventually led to the development of Kibblestone Scout Camp, which attracts visitors from all parts of the world.

Susie Cooper, pictured in the 1960s, was another woman pottery designer whose work combined originality with elegance. From 1929 she ran her own company and established her famous Crown Works at Burslem adjacent to Wood and Sons, her main suppliers of white ware. After a takeover in 1966 she worked for the Wedgwood group for 20 years until she retired to the Isle of Man.

When Josiah Wedgwood and Sons celebrated the firm's bicentenary as potters in 1959, an exhibition of Wedgwood ware was dispayed Selfridge's, the London store. Deputy Chairman Sir John Wedgwood, right, is seen showing a gravy boat to Selfridge's buyer Jack Wings.

As the notice beside her proclaimed, 13-year-old Evelyn Bailey was known as the Potteries Prodigy because she displayed a remarkable talent for throwing pots. She is seen here in the schoolyard at Glass Street School, Hanley, in 1930, at the potter's wheel owned by her grandfather, who taught both Evelyn and her sister in the craft. He also made a small kiln for the girls to fire their ware. Photograph loaned by Mrs Jean Keeling, of Derby.

Lord Mayor Jim Evans had a smashing time when he ceremonially broke up a number of flawed Spode plates in 1967. The company produced 900 of the commemorative pieces to mark the 900th anniversary of Westminster Abbey. Looking on in the Lord Mayor's Parlour at Stoke are Spode's managing director Spencer Copeland and Town Clerk Keith Robinson.

Potters on Film

Pottery workers on the screen? Yes, and rather more than just a fleeting glance in a clip of newsreel. A Pottery Girl's Romance was a full-blown drama of the silent days, featuring an all-local cast. It was shown in 1918. Nearly 30 years later the Central Office of Information made a dramatised documentary entitled The Five Towns for the big screen. Again, the cast was drawn almost exclusively from local talent. And there were potbank scenes on television in 1985 in a four-part adaptation of Arnold Bennett's Anna of the Five Towns on BBC2. The Gladstone Pottery Museum at Longton provided an ideal location.

Paintresses get on with their work while being filmed for a television programme in the 1960s. Over the years pottery workers have become used to the presence of TV cameras in the workshop, for both documentary films and drama.

Early workshop scene in the silent film A Pottery Girl's Romance, which was produced with a local cast and shown at Burslem Picture Palace in 1918. The heroine Mabel (played by Miss D Vickers) is the girl with smouldering eyes on the right.

Mabel has an admiring colleague named John (S Baddeley), who gives her a firm handclasp as they leave the potbank.

John senses there's trouble afoot as the bullying foreman Matt (A E Green) and his confederate Percy (H Hood) depart from the works in deep conversation.

Percy seeks out Mabel and, using a pretext, persuades her to go with him to a quiet spot at the back of a potbank.

Mabel soon realises she has been duped, but Percy wrestles her to the ground.

Enter the villain Matt, who tries to force his attentions on Mabel but finds she isn't easy prey.

Inevitably, the hero John comes to the rescue and gives the foreman a good hiding.

John is clearly going to be Mabel's man, although the pottery girl herself gets the sack from her job. Before the film ends there's more excitement when Mabel and her mother are rescued from a fire and the bullying Matt is shot by a different woman.

Life in a potbank was seen in cinemas round the world in 1947 in a half-hour dramatised documentary film called Five Towns. Made by the Central Office of Information, it showed a typical Potteries family both at home and at work, using a cast of nearly all local actors. The locations were a terraced house in Penkhull New Road, Stoke, the works of Crown Staffordshire China at Fenton and Wedgwoods. In this scene the father, played by Wilfred Hughes, is seen working in the sliphouse.

This is one of the two daughters in the household, a cup handler played by Winifred Hammond.

This picture shows Mary Blakeman, in the part of Aunt Florrie, taking expert advice on the job of a putter-up. Until making this fim, Mary had never been on a potbank in spite of her local upbringing. The film was shown at a number of North Staffordshire cinemas. These included the Danilo at Stoke, where Mary made a personal appearance on stage.

Kitchener Ridgeway, a genuine pottery oven firemen, testing the temperature in an oven at the Crown Staffordshire works.

Kathleen Hyde, in the role of a paintress, played another daughter in the Potteries family. Kathleen, then in her teens, worked as a copy typist in the Sentinel editorial department and later in life became well known as Sentinel Woman's Editor Kath Gosling.

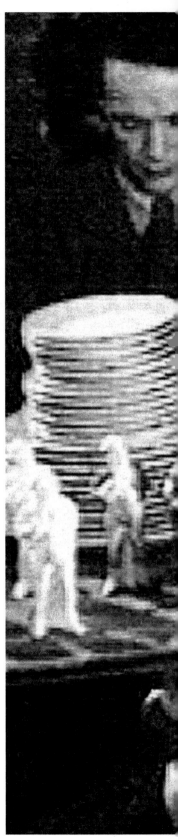

This scene, shot at Wedgwoods at Barlaston, shows the son of the family (played by Arthur Glover) checking an electric kiln. This modern setting contrasted with the traditional practices at the Crown Staffordshire works.

A genuine paintress pictured at work decorating a large vase. As the film was made in 1947, all the decorated ware was for the export market, as home sales were restricted to white ware by post-war austerity rules until 1952.

Henry begins the tour of the works with Anna as a worker passes by with a board of jugs. All these scenes were shot at the Gladstone Pottery Museum in Longton, formerly a pottery works.

Looking down on the courtyard as placers move in and out of the large bottle oven on the right. The outer wall of the oven is called the hovel, with the kiln built inside it.

Arnold Bennett's Bursley (Burslem) came back to the television screen in 1985 when BBC2 presented Anna of the Five Towns in four 50-minute episodes. In this series of pictures, Anna Tellwright (played by Linsey Beauchamp) is shown around a typical potbank by Henry Mynors (Peter Davison).

Anna takes in the bleak scenery at a 19th-century potbank, with smoke billowing from one of the ovens. Arnold Bennett describes pottery processes in his Five Towns novels.

Anna, a woman with a considerable fortune, listens intently as a pottery worker explains the intricacies of his job.

A paintress demonstrates her skills in another scene from Anna of the Five Towns, shown on BBC2 in 1985. The four-part adaptation was written by John Harvey and directed by Martyn Friend. The producer was Colin Rogers.